Praises for
WOKE

"Do yourselves a favor and read Stevie's latest book. As usual, he delivers huge value to entrepreneurs looking to be inspired to live their best life, connected to their purpose, their faith, their families, and their communities."

Jared Turner,
President/COO Young Living

This book moves us in reading as Spike Lee and Jordan Peele have for us in film. It gives proverbial meaning to School Daze's "Wake-Up" scene. Well done, Mr. Baggs. Well done.

Trina E. Braxton,
Entrepreneur and Talk Show Host

"Mr. Stevie Baggs, Jr. inspires his audiences to walk in their truth in a very authentic and powerful way!

His message is a wake up call for the many that are ready to take their lives to the next level and make success happen with a sense of urgency!"

Dr. Ona Brown,
The Message Midwife/Speaker Coach/Trainer/Author

Stevie Baggs, Jr. is one of the most brilliant minds of our time. Through sports, literature, and entrepreneruship, he's elevated melanated people while teaching and inspiring the masses.

Jamila Mustafa,
On Air Personality and Speaker
(ESPN, iHeart Radio, BET Networks, and MTV Networks)

Stevie Baggs, Jr. is the epitome of a king. A true brother who uplifts, enlightens, educates and spreads true love. He speaks life into the lives of many. He gives hope to the hopeless. He embodies strength, unwavering focus that I for one admire.

It is impossible to be around him and not leave better than you were before he graced you with his presence. I am excited about this book and grateful to call him a friend.

Sammie,
R & B Singer

Woke

A DICITONARY FOR THE CONSCIOUS MIND

Stevie Baggs, Jr.

13TH & JOAN

WOKE. Copyright © 2019 by Shakespeare Enterprises LLC. All rights reserved. No part of this publication may be reproduced, distributed, or transmitted in any form or by any means, including photocopying, recording, or other electronic or mechanical methods, without the prior written permission of the publisher, except in the case of brief quotations embodied in critical reviews and certain other noncommercial uses permitted by copyright law. For permission requests, write to the publisher, addressed "Attention: Permissions Coordinator," 500 N. Michigan Avenue, Suite #600, Chicago, IL 60611.

13th & Joan books may be purchased for educational, business or sales promotional use. For information, please email the Sales Department at sales@13thandjoan.com.

Printed in the U.S. A.
First Printing, October 2019
Library of Congress Cataloging-in-Publication Data has been applied for.

ISBN: 978-1-7331313-5-3 (Hardcover)
ISBN: 978-1-953156-12-9 (Paperback)

Dedication

This book is dedicated to the conscious thinker.

You never have to feel alone again.

WE NOW HAVE PROOF!!

You can *only* be awakened to follow your journey towards consciousness after *acknowledging* and decomposing the first accepted *lie*.

— *Stevie Briggs, Jr.*

Preface: An Open Letter to the Sleepers

> You can only be awakened to follow your journey towards consciousness after acknowledging and decomposing the first accepted lie.
>
>
> — Stevie Briggs, Jr.

ARE YOU AWAKE OR ASLEEP?

As effortless as this question may sound, the true answer for each of us is more complex in nature than you might have once believed. There is a remarkable difference between the way you experience life while awake versus being asleep. I write this message as a byproduct of my mission to equip you with the capacity to consider the difference between the two. I would also venture to say that the vast majority of us experience life while sleeping. My humble plea is for you to consider the fullness of your current circumstance of potential slumber. I, like most, have journeyed through life while asleep. The most prolific consideration to this end is that I was unaware. I was living life and engaging in each day with eyes wide shut. There is no shame in having done so. When we arrive into the world, our bodies tell us to sleep as it fights to recover from the forced myriad of information fed to us from the powers that be. These powers that I speak of determine who we are destined to become and send us inescapable messages about how we must characterize ourselves. Subscribing to the notion that anyone other than you should have the insurmountable power to tell you who you are and what you will become is unjust, but we have all been there. Today, based on experience and awakening, I can proudly proclaim that life has more to offer you when you are awakened.

WAKING UP IS A CHOICE

Let me be clear in saying that I have come to terms with the fact that not everyone desires to wake up. Doing so is a choice that we either select, or allow to be selected on our behalves. Making the decision to wake up, also means making the decision to heighten your consciousness. The infinite value in this space is that you possess a willingness and desire to experience life more abundantly. Over the years, my patterns of thinking have evolved such that I have become more present. I also realize that my presence is a present to the universe. This same sentiment rings true for each of us. We have been placed here to serenade the world with our gifts and talents. To this end, we are in no position to offer of ourselves if we are not awake. Doing so is a disservice and demonstration of a lack of stewardship over all that we are destined to be.

It pains me to bear witness to those who endeavor to walk through life, accepting only the truths that we have been given. There is more. The world has more to offer when we walk in the power and motivations of our highest vibration. This can only be achieved while chasing consciousness.

WAKING UP HURTS LIKE HELL

I would be remiss if I did not tell you that choosing to walk while awake is also a choice to relentlessly ignore the pain of consciousness. Choosing to discover truth is indicative of relinquishment of the process of indoctrination that has been leveraged to control our minds, our bodies and our spirits. There is so much to unpack and unlearn. The process to unlearn and relearn, and to open compartments in our mind that might have forever remained closed, takes work and grit and diligence. This process is not for the faint of heart or the weak of mind. The prize becomes your presence. Experiencing life in abundance becomes accessible and a heightened awareness of your existence is among the greatest gifts that you can give you yourself.

CONSCIOUSNESS IS A DESTINATION

Today, one of my greatest joys is knowing that I have allowed myself to serve as a vessel and light for consciousness without limits. This is a role that I don't take for granted, and it is rooted in UNIVERSAL PURPOSE. If you remember nothing else that I have written to you, never forget that YOU are the most POWERFUL being that YOU will ever experience. Your destiny and ability to engage with people and the world around you, whether awake or asleep, will always be your choice. Now, I ask, what will you do with it? I dare you to wake up and experience the sweetest fruit of life. The world needs you.

-SBJ

Acknowledgements

GIVING THANKS HAS become more effortless for me as the years pass, but as I continue to evolve, I recognize that thankfulness is a rarity in our world. I would like to start by paying homage to the generations of visionaries, philosophers, and intellectual giants that have paved the way for us to have mental/spiritual autonomy. We live in a society where thinking differently can make you an outcast and sometimes a target.

I'm so thankful that I have FAMILY, FRIENDS, PEERS, and MENTORS that have ALL seen what being "WOKE" truly means to me and who respect that part of my journey.

To 13th & Joan, your contribution has been tremendous, and I thank you. We have much more work to do!

To my lovely Queen, your opulence, support, and spirit fuels me daily.

To my daughter, we have a bond that will never be broken.

To my parents in humanity and divinity, your guidance will always be treasured.

I'd also like to thank you, the reader, for your support; and I know that if you open your heart to truth and not tradition, that you will grasp something majestic from this book that will empower you to transcend your life and levels of consciousness.

Lastly, I'd like to thank the Universal One, the Grand Architect of celestial consciousness, The God of all things visible and invisible. If it had not been for this calling, I would not be able to invoke a vision of love, wisdom, inner-standing, health, wealth, prosperity, favor, peace, patience, might, anointing, integrity, and truth. TO ALL OF MANKIND.

Table of Contents

EPIGRAPH

PREFACE: AN OPEN LETTER TO THE SLEEPERS

I: PRE CONSCIOUSNESS

AWAKENING #1: ONE MUST LEAVE THE SHORE TO CROSS THE OCEAN

FEATURED CONCEPTS & DEFINITIONS
The NUMBER 9
Television

II: POST CONSCIOUSNESS

AWAKENING #2: CONSCIOUSNESS DETERMINES QUALITY OF LIFE

ACKNOWLEDGEMENTS

INTRODUCTION: INTELLIGENCE ASKS QUESTIONS

Pulpit
Good Morning
Death
Life
Heart
Foundarity
Star
Seedless

THE PRE-CONSCIOUS AFFIRMATION

FEATURED CONCEPTS & DEFINITIONS
Authority
Fly (First Love Yourself) & AIR (Access, Influence and Resources)

UGLY (Understand God Loves You)
Masses (Be Careful When You Follow...)
Media (Multi Ethnic Devastation In America)
The Seasons
Black
Blanco
NIGGA

THE POST CONSCIOUS AFFIRMATION

III: SUPER CONSCIOUSNESS

AWAKENING #3: TRANSFORMATION IS AN INSIDE JOB

STD
Fellowship
Corpse
Months of the Year
FICO Score
Racism

FEATURED CONCEPTS & DEFINITIONS
SWAG
KID

THE SUPER CONSCIOUS AFFIRMATION

IV: ETYMOLOGY, WORDPLAY AND PHRASES THAT ENLIGHTEN

A 360 Degree Perspective
Past, Present, Future
Step Into the Light
A Righteous Path
Higher Order Thinking
The Power of Invisibility
Ego vs. Emotion
Farm or Pharmacy
Scare the Hell Out of Them
Career Goals
Paper Chaser vs. Purpose Chaser
I Want to Be Rich
Bound, Broken and Wrapped in Chains
Workaholic
We Are the World

A Time for All Seasons
High Off Emotions
Subconscious
Say it Loud
Follow the Leader
Truth vs. Tradition
All Power
Relax, Relate, Release
Love and Let Go
Give and You Shall Receive
A Wealthy Mindset
Law and Order
GUN
24 Hour Balance
The Real Bag
Charitist
Let Your Soul Glow
Run and Tell That

Witty Are We?
Personal Business
Reign
The Sun Will Come Out
A Bird's Eye View
The Pleasure Principle
Imagine That
Real Recognizes Real
The Shape
A Queen Indeed
Stand Corrected
Programming and Beliefs
Holidays
Worship the Source Not the Resource
Sweat
Misunderstanding

EPILOGUE: EMPTY MINDS MUST BE FILLED

AFTERWORD: OPENED MINDS OPEN DOORS

POSTSCRIPT: UNWRAPPING THE GIFT OF CURIOSITY

WOKE 360

WOKE 360: 21 DAY CHALLENGE

ABOUT THE AUTHOR

CONNECT WITH STEVIE BAGGS, JR. ON SOCIAL MEDIA

Your past thinking is *dust,* your future thinking is *clay*, yet, your present thinking is a *gift* and we must mold it accordingly.

— Stevie Briggs, Jr.

Introduction: Intelligence Asks Questions

> "To be or not to be must never be the question. You must know with certainty that you already are."
>
> — Stevie Briggs, Jr.

IF YOU HAD the power to ask a single question that would allow you to be enlightened by the absolute truth, what question would you ask? I would venture to say that this is a loaded question, but one that must be answered nonetheless. As opposed to asking a single question, I resolve that you must resolve to ask many. Not only must you ask questions about the things that you are curious about, but you must also ask questions on a consistent basis to acquire new information to dissect on your own terms. And, regardless of whether you believe the act of questioning the world around you is simple or complex, the way in which you inquire about everything can easily be streamlined. In grade school, you were likely introduced to the 5W's (Who? What? When? Where? and Why?). This strategy was said to be most useful for information gathering or problem solving. To live the greatest life that you are capable of living, it is my belief that you must gather information and solve problems repeatedly. Assuming this stance can lead to great victories, and more importantly, increased levels of consciousness.

As we unravel this process throughout this book, it is my hope that you make life changing connections between the information that is presented to you and your ability to dissect it; and that you are led to look deeper into the words that you speak while recognizing them as triggers for your awakening. Your words have infinite power. Moreover, your mind has a capacity that could potentially be untapped.

UNIVERSAL TRUTHS

Universal truths are inarguable..like oxygen. Oxygen doesn't care what color you are, what religion you align with, how much money you have in your bank account. Some people may have a different word for it, but gravity does not care about your ethnicity your creed, your degrees, your neglect, nor your wins in this game called life. If you fall off of a building, gravity is going to let you know that it is real. Inarguably, any human born has been in the womb for 9 months. You may have premature babies, but the human system is set up for a woman to produce life in 9 months. Can you control your heartbeat? Does your heart need your permission to beat? No! It's that type of ineffability that makes you realize the tremendous power of universal truths that supersedes tradition.

The super-consciousness is something that we will dive into deeper in the text, but when you connect with that, and are able to function in society, you have truly found peace. I have determined that many don't have the ability to unlearn and relearn what they've been programmed and taught as truth due to exposure or the lack thereof. This factor is one of the most disheartening things to consider. It's a beautiful thing that one can be committed to something and proclaim it as truth, but also sad that one can be committed to something to their detriment. It really is honorable that we can be so spiritually connected to religion, the way we eat, our marriages and family structures; but disheartening that once you are exposed to an inarguable truth it is often challenging to change the old behavior or be(LIE)f. We've been programmed to remain enslaved to things that block purpose, but we will still remain loyal to those things because society, tradition, or our particular CULTure told us and taught us the way.

One of the most difficult shifts is trying to teach the people you love the most about things that can help them. Far too often due to systematic conditioning they don't want to let go of their old behavior or comfort levels. Asertaining higher levels of awareness has been calcified. You have to be strong enough to let them go. We must remember that the truth hurts, but it shall also set you free. We are in an age now, due to technology, that many are called to universal truth or can access it in some way, yet everyone won't choose to do so. The greatest way to bring folks to your level of Super Consciousness is to model it in the way you live your life. You must also remember to never forget to lean on UNIVERSAL TRUTHS to substantiate your position. TRUTH doesn't have to be validated by ignorance. In my first book, "Greater Than The Game," there is a chapter entitled, "FAITH," and it stands for Foundation Abiding In Truth Highup. I would venture to say that my evolution and growth has taken me to a place that surpasses faith. Now as a Super Conscious being,

I KNOW that God, Yahweh, the Grand Architect, or the Universal One is real. This is no longer a belief.

WHO?

My name is Stevie Baggs, Jr. and I AM WOKE! For me, the term WOKE is a state of consciousness that welcomes the highest frequencies of energy from which to vibrate.

WHAT?

I am not the first thinker to speak or reproduce information about consciousness. Sigmund Freud's concepts of consciousness were widely adopted. It is my belief that the creation of such avenues for the transfer of information and thought by those who have had similar life experiences, can add context to the terms of enlightenment.

Whereas most books are written to transport a multitude of messages, many subscribing to a myriad of thoughts, this book has but one purpose…To transform your thinking. My experiences have served as the backdrop for the evolution of my mind, body, and spirit. It is from this perspective that I have been empowered and enabled to approach the emergence of thoughts and ideas presented to you in this book. And, while my call to action is not to implore you to think as I do or to simply adopt my truth as your own, I am asking you to step outside of what you have known to be true to analyze it for yourself. I dare you to create a universal truth that is based solely upon your life's experiences and not only what you have been fed by society at large. This book and its contents requests that you allow yourself to engage in moments of deep, transformational thought and heightened conscious amidst your experiences.

WHEN?

There is no time like the present! Don't waste another second of your life wondering what's beyond the veil. All you have to do is open your mind and be willing to level up and see for yourself that now is the time for something higher/deeper.

WHERE?

We have been taught to look without so much that we often times don't look within. Once you go within, you will see that the next level of awakening was always there. INSIDE!

WHY?

The result of reading this book is the transformation of your internal compass. I challenge you to make careful, intelligent, and deliberate decisions.

You may choose to call this book many things, but I have resolved to refer to it as a dictionary for the conscious mind. Should you decide to enter, know that you do so at the risk of elevating your consciousness. I dare you to turn the page.

One:
Pre-Consciousness

> We are gravely mistaken to believe that we can solve our trials with the same level of consciousness in which they were constructed.
>
> — *Stevie Baggs Jr.*

PRE-CONSCIOUS CAN BE paralleled to the consciousness you have as a child. In this state, you are molded and provided with a set of beliefs that you adopt as your truth because you have been told them to be accordingly.

The sun desires to *rise*.
Water desires to *flow*.
The mind desires to *inquire*.

— *Stevie Baggs, Jr.*

Awakening #1:
One Must Leave the Shore to Cross the Ocean

THE WHITE SAND and illuminated skies of Pompano Beach, Florida served as the illustrious backdrop for my adolescent years. And although our town was noted for the presence of the beach, crossing the railroad tracks meant stepping into what some would refer to as, societal imposed disparity. All residents in the city did not live equally. In some areas, exposure was limited to proximity and access to income. For many, that also meant limiting sets of beliefs solely based on lack of access to information. I spent my days amidst the pews of a Pentecostal church. Best described as strict and laced with tradition, I was locked into a mindset and process of thought that had been cultivated by the way that things had always been. I can recall so vividly, attending church on Sunday, Sunday school, and bible study on Wednesdays. The services were long, as we were guided by a higher power and not hours on the clock. When we were not in service, we spent time in fellowship with the other members.

I was a Jr. Deacon, and very much a product of what I had been taught. From reading hymnals to playing the drums, singing in the choir and rendering devotions, I was ingrained in both the practice and the culture. My childhood was protected, and at times, exposure to things that were considered secular was limited. I hadn't even been exposed to secular music until at least ten years of age. The culture and community taught me to be of sound ethical standards and provided me with a good moral compass. I would also venture to say that discipline and even drive were byproducts of my rearing. Conviction for what was right and wrong was ever present and the demonstration of passion for the things that were of importance was deeply ingrained in my spirit. In this era, I accepted many answers about the world around me and my disposition in it as my truth, simply because it was tradition. I did not venture to inquire, research, or test anything that was presented to me in this space. My truth was simply the aftermath of what I saw. Respectively, if your truth is only what you see or only what you are conditioned or manipulated to receive, then you will remain in a box. I had not yet ventured beyond the beaches, but would later come to recognize that there were new levels of conscious available to me that would allow me to inquire about the world around me, and to use curiosity as an internal GPS for who and what I would dare to become.

NINE

NINE
/nīn/

The sum of three times three.

WOKE DEFINITION:
The number nine is symbolic for a myriad of reasons. Hair has the ability to coil into the number nine. We are in the womb for

9 months. This means that life comes full circle, in a nine month span. Most notably, another symbol for the circle is the number 360. If you add 3+6+0, it equals 9. If you cut 360 in half, 180 remains. 1+8+0=9. Half of 180 equals 90. 9+0=9. Half of 90, is 45. 4+5=9. And half of 45 is 22.5. 2+2+5=9. Nine is an ether number.

TELEVISION

TEL·E·VI·SION
/ˈteləˌviZHən/

Visual images and sounds transferred to a receiver from a screen.

WOKE DEFINITION:
Television is a form of programming and can be used to communicate messages that promote an intended agenda. We must act with haste to examine the motives of the programming that we choose to consume. It is imperative that you search for deeper meaning and understanding by asking yourself if the agenda of

the programming is to your benefit or detriment? All messaging has not been created equal. To this end, some messaging has been established to devalue and oppress designated groups of people. The acceptance of predetermined messaging as your truth is harmful and has lasting effects. Under no circumstances should you underestimate your intake. Television is a very powerful form of programming.

In the middle of the word television, you can find the letters "L" and "I". This can also be categorized as TE-LIE-VISION. The programming, when unraveled and dissected, reveals a multitude of lies and fictitious concepts fed as truth. You must dig deeper to discover the factors that are not real. If I control the image, I control the ideas. If I control the ideas, I control the thinking. If I control the thinking, I control the actions.

Television and religion shape your belief system. In the middle of both reLIgion and beLIEf is L-I-E—lie. If we shall know the truth, and the truth is supposed to set us free, my question to all is, why aren't we free? Do you really feel like you're free in your mind? Do you feel free in the way you think? Most would answer unequivocally, NO. And the reason most don't feel free is because we've been LIED to. Remember...Freedom has nothing to do with shackles and handcuffs. Harriett Tubman was quoted as saying, "I freed thousands of slaves. I could have freed thousands more if they only knew they were slaves." The worst bondage is found in the mind.

PULPIT

PUL·PIT
/ˈpəlˌpit/
A platform utilized by religious figures to teach and inform.

WOKE DEFINITION:

PULL PIT

If you are taught from sources and circumstances that are meant to oppress you, as opposed to lifting you up, have you been exposed to a **PULL or PIT?** If the speaker has been indoctrinated and not empowered, the words and intentions behind them do not have the power or potential to help you ascend.

GOOD MORNING

GOOD MORN·ING
/good ˈmôrniNG/
An exclamation or phrase used as a greeting when one arises in what is considered the morning hours of the day.

WOKE DEFINITION:
The term *morning*, or as spelled in Canada/Europe, *mourning*, when heard in the universe, could plant the wrong seed. Mourning is to mourn the dead. If this is the case, then we could potentially speak death over the start of our day, as opposed to life. Consider the term GREAT RISING/GRAND AWAKENING. This denotes that there is the expectancy of energy and vibrations that uplift and inspire.

Death
Life
Heart

In the middle of each of these words are other words that tell a story. In Death is EAT and what we eat physically or spiritually will determine our life or death. In the middle of the word Life is IF how many people do you know that live a (what if) life? As oppose to being thankful for the gift called now. In the Middle of the word heart is EAR. I urge you to be mindful of the things that we internalize through or ear gate, because toxic thoughts create toxic outcomes. However, tonic thoughts create tonic outcomes.

STAR

STAR
/stär/
A celestial body or fixed illumination in the sky.

WOKE DEFINITION:

S: Seeker

T: Teacher

A: And

R: Reacher

IF YOU SPELL THIS SAME WORD BACKWARDS, it is the word *RATS*.

SEEDLESS

SEED·LESS
/ˈsēdləs/
A fruit that bears no seeds.

WOKE DEFINITION:
If there is an object that is said to have life but bears no seed, then it can be derived that it has no soul. Consider and caution your consumption of people, places, and things that bear no seeds.

Affirmation #1:
CONNECTIONS

I AM intrinsically connected to life.

The universe always provides for me.

Prosperity flows through me.

Two: Post Consciousness

> **Elevated consciousness dictates an elevated life experience.**
> — Stevie Biggs Jr.

Post Consciousness can be categorized as a by product of your Pre-Consciousness. This state of being is the evolution of your truth based upon your exposure and your experiences.

One's *journey* to be whole can only be walked from an internal path.

— Stevie Briggs, Jr.

Awakening #2:
Consciousness Determines Quality of Life

AT THE AGE of 21, I was playing football at the highest level possible. I had proven to myself, and the world, that my abilities were worthy of being paid for the results that I was capable of producing on the field. My collegiate years had served as the backdrop for my confidence. After being awarded as a 3X All-American and receiving the prestigious Black College Player of the Year award, a notable accolade previously acquired by the likes of Jerry Rice, Walter Peyton, and Michael Strayhan, I didn't question my abilities. With clearly what I believed to be a well defined future, I approached each game and opportunity as if my future depended on it; and it did. And, even though my draft had not been what I had hoped, I was there and believed, without question, that I deserved to be there on the field playing a game that had become synonymous with purpose in my soul. I thirsted to create the life that I had always dreamed of, on and off the field.

Amidst the immense travel that playing at this level afforded, I also discovered that my opportunities for exposure to new people, places, and things evolved.

My quest to expand who I was becoming on the field was just as profound as it was off the field. The more exposure that I gained in the world, the more information I yearned to acquire. My curiosity was peaked in so many ways. The process of evolution led to the transformation of my thoughts. The way that I received and accepted information differed from the way in which I received it as a young boy growing up in Florida. Somewhere along the way, I let go of my acquisition and acceptance of information solely based on tradition, and opened my hands to truths based upon my experiences. Things that once made sense, no longer; and eventually, I let go of religion and opened my hands to righteousness. That was the stamp of my post consciousness. In this space, I viewed the world differently and found comfort in doing so. That same discovery of self would prove more meaningful in the days to come.

The illustrious city of Detroit had earned the title of home in my heart and the physical disposition. The more acclimated I felt to the city, the more I visualized my future there. In late August 2004, I was at the final practice prior to the team's departure for our last preseason game. That day, I had not taken the sun shining for granted and for whatever reason, I even appreciated the heat that warmed the grass on the field. It was a sign of replenishment and prosperity. Practice had gone well, and I looked forward to the next day at the game. Unbeknownst to me, I would never play another down for the Detroit Lions.

While jogging off the field, the TURK came over to request my playbook. The Turk is the staff member who is responsible for informing players that they have been cut from the team.

Both his presence and his request took my breath away. I had not seen this moment coming. Never in a million years would I have guessed that my career with the Detroit Lions would end on that day, and in that way. To say that I was blindsided would be an understatement. In that moment, my entire life flashed behind my eyes. My heart was met with great uncertainty. Would I ever be able to play football again? Did I need to get out and get a job? I had invested my entire life into the game and achieved a level that only 1% of the people ever get to do. Was it possible that all of the work and grit and politics that I endured was for not?

In retrospect during my moments of reflection, I realized that I had never even considered the business of the sport. Football had captivated my heart and soul for so many years that I believed my purpose to be attached to it. I recognized that I needed to find something else to consume my thoughts and my energy so that I would not take ownership of the sense of emptiness and fear that had managed to sink in. I fought to remind myself that I was greater than the game and that I had been created to aspire to many levels of greatness throughout my lifetime. This is true for each of us.

New levels of consciousness have allowed me to recognize that football is not synonymous with purpose. The hard truth is that football was a game that only allows each player to be as good as the last play. After resolving to dig deeper, I began to use my mind and consciousness to transcend even the game that I love most and to discard fear. Leaning on fear, and not recognizing that I had so much ahead of me, I did not know the worth of my consciousness. I had not locked in on it.

Today, the single most transformative revelation that has occupied my entire being is, such, that fear and God can't occupy the same space. That day on the field, I thought that my life was over. Little did I know that it was the beginning of a new season that would empower me to establish a message that could grow wings to fly all over the world, not just the field.

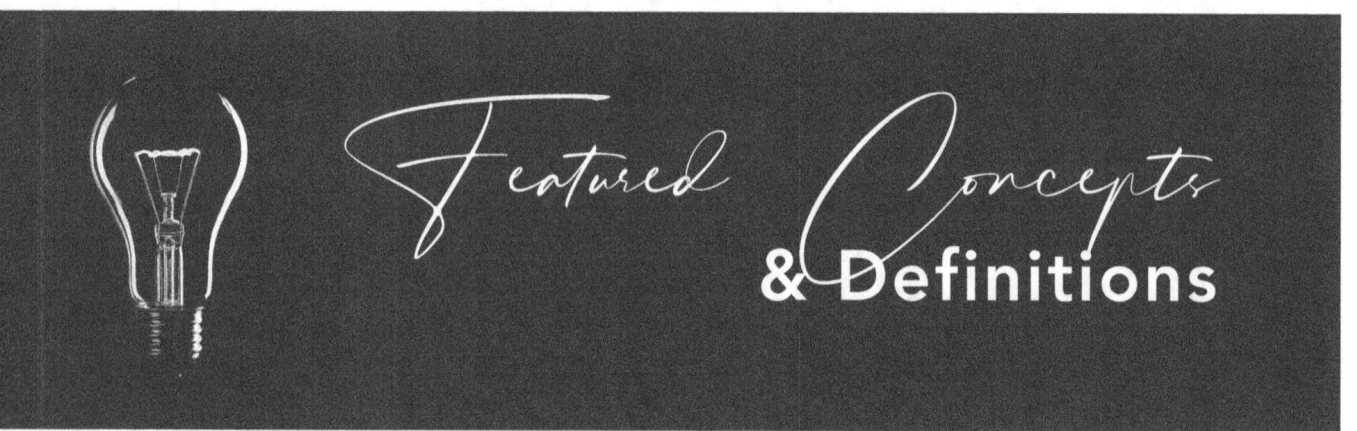

AUTHORITY

AU·THOR·I·TY
/əˈTHôrədē/

The power or right.

WOKE DEFINITION:
The prefix to the word Authority is Author. When you author something, you give it authority/power to take flight and manifest.

Fly (First Love Yourself)

AIR (Access, Influence and Resources)

UGLY (Understand God Loves You)

Masses (Be Careful When You Follow...)

MEDIA (Multi Ethnic Devastation In America)

The Seasons
Winter, Spring, Summer, and Fall are all seasons, but there is a DUE season when it's your time to take flight. In the Summer, you sum up all of your harvest...In the Fall, you become a great steward over the harvest from the summer... If so, in the Winter, you WIN.

BLACK

BLACK
/blak/
Owing to the absence of or complete absorption of light. A member of a dark-skinned people.

WOKE DEFINITION:
If you separate the word *black,* it's B-LACK. B can not stand alone. You "B" in "Lack" when you call yourself black.

When you call yourself black, you are in lack of your universal truths. Being in lack is a state of mind, and more profoundly, it comes to fruition when you allow yourself to be programmed with names and statuses that don't belong to you, and those that were not created to empower you. Why not refer to yourself as indigenouse, aboriginated, or melanated? If you are from the motherland, but you mimic everyone from the other land, this denotes that you are in lack.

Also consider that in Latin, the word *black* is defined as colorless. We are not a colorless people. Melanin bears color.

BLANC
/blanc/

In the French language, means white.

BLANCO
/blanco/

In the spanish language, means white.

WOKE DEFINITION:

Blanco means white. Respectively, the term blanc means white. The names do not dictate the actual color. Why speak untruths into existence if they are not the most powerful characterization of who you are? Instead of calling yourself black, consider calling yourself melanated/indigenious/aboriginal/carbon. Change the narrative.

NIGGA

NIG·GA
/ˈnigə/

Informal or offensive. Often used to negatively define and oppress a group of people.

WOKE DEFINITION:
N: *Never*

I: *Ignorant*

G: *Getting*

G: *Goals*

A: *Accomplished*

DEPRESSION

DE·PRES·SION
/dəˈpreSH(ə)n/
Feelings of dejection that often lead to despondency.

WOKE DEFINITION:
In the term depression, the word *press* appears. You also have the terms *re and pre*. These terms can serve as predictors of the energy that you will, speak or allow into your life. Everything goes back to your consumption. The by-product of your consumption is your production. If a person is consuming bio-available nutrients and water and getting rest, it is possible that he or she has the ability to run a marathon and ride a bike for 40-50 miles. In many instances, we could assume that this person is consum-

ing entities that are beneficial for them on a cellular level. From a mental perspective, if you tell me what a person thinks, I can tell you what they have likely been consuming with their minds and what kind of people surround them.

Let us also consider the autonomic nervous system. This system automatically functions without you telling it what to do. Your heart, your liver, your pancreas, your kidneys, and your colon, are all organs that work automatically. The central nervous system tells you to speak, to walk, and to clap. If you are consuming nutrients on a cellular level, and on an autonomic nervous system level, then your overall performance or output will be better. Everything goes back to what you're consuming…your mouth, your hands, your ears. You have two of everything, but you have one mouth. What are you putting into it and what are you saying out of it?

These connections in no way negate the true effects of depression and its associated causes. The purpose of thi sdefinition is simply to draw your attention to the correlation between input and output. We are ever reproducing what we consume

Post Consciousness Affirmation

I AM aligned with energy and prosperity.

I attract and reproduce vibrations that revitalizes me.

I manifest what I will and work for it with ease.

My reality is in infinite harmony with the divinity of time, talent and treasure.

Three:
Super Consciousness

> Remain faithful to the calling for higher consciousness
>
> — *Stevie Briggs Jr.*

SUPER-CONSCIOUS denotes that you are open to the acquisition of more information, and your behaviors directly align with new levels of connections made. In this space, you thrive in society against the commonality of untruths that you may be exposed to without being influenced by them. Vibration at this level requires a willingness to change and redirect you actions as a result of the newly acquired information.

The act of seeking consciousness is the highest form of revolution.

— Stevie Briggs, Jr.

Awakening #3: Transformation is an Inside Job

AS I CONTINUE to evolve my thinking and my conscious, I realized that it worked when I got invited to speak at Oxford University in Clemson and the Boys and Girls Club in the hood in Atlanta, and the message and the intention is the same. To have the space to share the same message to a multitude of people and it be valid in all spaces.

Super Conscious moments happen everyday for me. I am always sharing thoughts so that others can think. You don't have to think like me…I just want you to THINK LIKE ME.

Never allow your mindset to be made up for you.

When I was able to combine my foundation and pre with post conscious experience, it got me to a place of super conscious. Now, speaking around the world and on television sets, I have a direct approach to how I work and interact with people. It gave me that much more GODFIDENCE in the ability that the universal God placed on my life.

If your thoughts only connect to one group of people, is that being a thought leader or are you a thought leader in one setting? The more that I grow, I have always wanted to make sure that I could connect to all hues...all ethnicities and backgrounds. Truth does not have an expiration date, nor does it need to be validated by ignorance.

I continue to evolve daily. When you truly become superconscious, you get to a space where the more you know, the more you realize what you don't know. This level of existence keeps you weak enough and hungry enough to hunt for more information. You can't feed a steak to a baby. If someone is a baby in their level of consciousness, they will not be able to chew or digest what is being fed to them. This train of thought is also true of our consciousness.

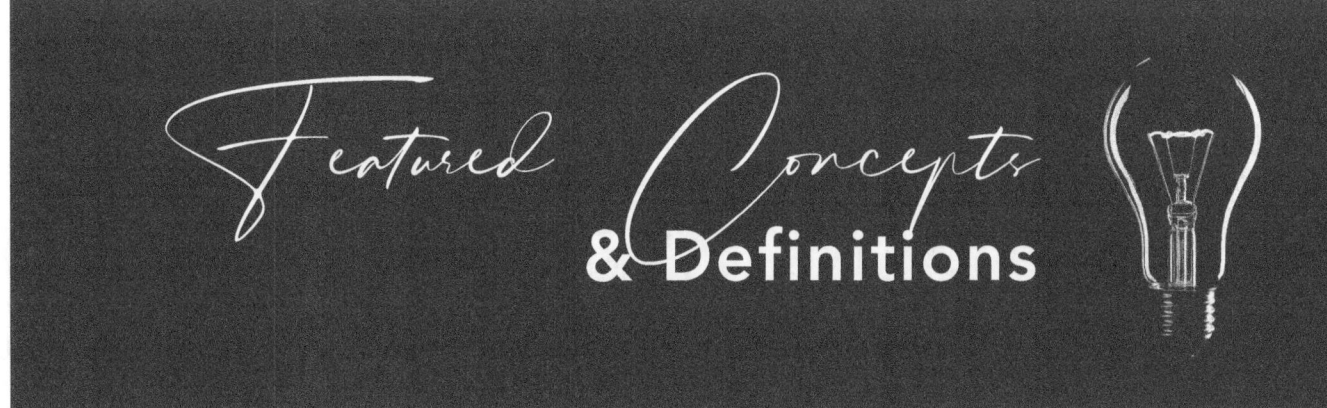

SWAG

SWAG
/swag/

A curtain or piece of fabric. The urban definition defers to a way in which one carries him or herself.

WOKE DEFINITION:
S: *Saved*
W: *With*
A: *Amazing*
G: *Grace*

KID

KID
/kid/
Most often categorized as a young person. This term is also used to reference a young goat.

WOKE DEFINITION:
It is unquestionable that children are the future. Accordingly, there is the power of life and death in the tongue. Speaking anything that remotely suggests that children can be classified as young goats is counterproductive. A young goat is also referred to as an ass. This is not synonymous with the prosperity that is sought for the future generations of the world.

STD

STD
/ˌes ˌtē ˈdē/
A disease that is transmitted through intercourse.

WOKE DEFINITION:

Are you concerned with what is passed to your soul from those that you encounter? Far too often, we consider the germs and disease that can be transmitted from physical contact with little to no regard about those same entities being transferred to our souls. In heightened consciousness, we must protect our souls and our bodies from poison and evil.

S: *Spiritually*
T: *Transmitted*
D: *Disease*

FELLOWSHIP

FEL·LOW·SHIP
/ˈfelōˌSHip/
Friendly association with those who have similar interests.

WOKE DEFINITION:
The ship brings thing to and from. The people gathering together is fellowship.

CORPSE

CORPSE
/kôrps/
A body that is no longer alive.

WOKE DEFINITION:
A dead body is referred to as a corpse because you are actually a CORPORATION. Your social security number makes you a corporation.

Months of the Year
Every month
January, February, March, April, May, June, July, September, October
Why in our months of the year
Deca is a 10.

FICO Score

RACISM

RAC·ISM
/ˈrāˌsizəm/
A belief that one's race is superior to another.

WOKE DEFINITION:
The war is not racism it is against

Racism is only a fraction of what we are fighting.

Everyone of your color is not of your kind. This means that there are greater forces implemented to separate us. When we consider racism, we must consider every angle of oppression attempted.

Super Conscious Affirmation

I AM Omnipresent.

I am energized and directed by one mind.

I approach each day amidst the highest margin of consciousness.

My subconscious basks in the realm of possibilities and wades in purpose.

I will think, learn, and analyze to arrive at my universal truths.

Four:
Etymology, Wordplay and Phrases That Enlighten

> Life can have no meaning in the absence of consciousness.
>
> — Stevie Briggs, Jr.

THE STANDARD definition of the word **ETYMOLOGY** refers to the study of the origin of words, as well as, how they have developed or evolved over time. By virtue of this definition, your curiosity should be piqued.

Consider The Following:

- How is it possible that a word's meaning be changed or evolved over time?
- Who are the powers that be, deemed conscious enough to determine how, when, and why the meaning of words with definitions adopted as universal truths change over time?

Your quest to deepen your understanding also means taking time to familiarize yourself with the roots of words to ensure that you are empowered to maintain definitions of words that are conducive to your patterns of thinking and your universal truths. If you agree that your words have power, then you have also discovered the need to know more about the words and phrases that you speak.

A 360 DEGREE PERSPECTIVE

The number nine has the ability to transform the disposition of our thoughts if we are willing to step outside of ourselves. Consider that if two people stood toe to toe with the number nine beneath them displayed on the floor, one on either side, each would see two different things. The person standing at the top of the number nine would see the number six. The person standing at the bottom of the number nine would see nine. If the person standing at the top made the decision to come to stand with the person who is viewing the nine from the bottom, then they would respectively see the same thing. The number nine is evolutionary in that, if we open ourselves up to the realm of increased consciousness, we can greater understand and appreciate the notion that everyone has adopted their truths based upon what they see and their experiences. To this end, the number nine is the amount of time that the ultimate evolution takes place. It is a powerful concept when you consider stepping outside of yourself to consider the dispositions of others. In this space, you recognize that your truth is your truth and you have the ability to attain an inverted and powerful perspective as you visualize a myriad of scenarios.

PAST, PRESENT, FUTURE

The past is dust, the future is clay; you must mold it with strategy and care to experience and multiply all your days.

STEP INTO THE LIGHT

How can you categorize yourself as the light of the world, but not seek to illuminate a path for others?

A RIGHTEOUS PATH

Master the avoidance of self-distraction to alleviate self-destruction.

HIGHER ORDER THINKING

Why would you be worried about making a living if you are unsure of the reason why you live?

THE POWER OF INVISIBILITY

Everything that you see with your eyes is supported by what you can't see with your eyes. This is a spiritual term. If you see flowers blooming, they are all supported by things you can't see, such as, water or air. Everything that you see with your eyes is supported by what you can't see.

EGO VS. EMOTION

Your number one enemy is not human.
The most profound enemy for a man is ego.
The most profound enemy for a woman is emotion.
Your number one enemy is not human and it is invisible.

FARM OR PHARMACY

If you close your eyes, you might be confused as to if the FARM or PHARM is being utilized. When you have that type of ambiguous language, it leads to dualities. It is imperative that you dig into studying the origins of words, the prefixes and suffixes, and the etymology behind it all. Exactness is what you are after.

SCARE THE HELL OUT OF THEM

The term *scare the hell out of them* has been established and defined with a negative connotation. An enlightened consciousness, opens an opportunity to ask if the removal of hell is a bad thing? If you scare the hell out of people, could it be possible that you have the opportunity and free space to add some heaven into them?

CAREER GOALS

Your career is what you are paid to do. Your purpose is what the universe or God created you to do.

PAPER CHASE VS. PURPOSE CHASE

There is a significant difference between *paper chasing* and *purpose chasing*. Purpose is everlasting and it can not run out. The stores of purpose are replenished by using more of it and being of service to more people through purpose. If chasing paper is your goal, it is possible that you stop chasing it after attaining a certain level of success or amount. Chasing paper can and will lead to stagnation. Chasing purpose leads to prosperity that can't be quantified. Whether you're 8 years old or 80 years old, the purpose chase is infinite in nature. When you recognize that money, like many resources is energy. If your purpose is leveraged, you will discover an abundance of resources as a reward for your stewardship over your most valuable gifts, such as your time, talent, and treasure. Money will always follow energy and purpose.

I WANT TO BE RICH

Focusing solely on the money leaves little to no room for determining the acquisition or retention of it. What purpose would have been served to have gained it and not possess the ability to keep it?

BOUND, BROKEN, AND WRAPPED IN CHAINS

Before a building is created, the creator must break ground. There are times in your life when being broken is the start of a new infrastructure.

WORKAHOLIC

Your goal must be to create work that facilitates wealth, not more work.

WE ARE THE WORLD

What they see is what they will be. What are you teaching the next generation about you?

A TIME FOR ALL SEASONS

A lot of people relate seasons in life that they go through; life correlates with season of peace or prosperity. I feel that a direct correlation of the four seasons they give. If you are a good steward over the summer, you'll win over winter. In the spring, talk about springing back into your blessing. There's also a season called dual season where sometimes…

HIGH OFF EMOTIONS

If egos and emotions are high, the presence of logic is unquestionably low.

SUBCONSCIOUS

Your subconscious gives life to your vision. If you resolve to not have vision, then what is the purpose of your living?

SAY IT LOUD

The greatest speech you will ever give is the life you live.

FOLLOW THE LEADER

Be careful when you follow the Masses, sometimes the *M* is silent.

TRUTH VS. TRADITION

When you become open to receive truth, never allow traditions to stand in the way.

ALL POWER

If you save one person, you have the power to save the world. If you damage one person, you have the power to damage the world.

RELAX, RELATE, RELEASE

The key word to consider in the word RELATIONSHIP is *relate*. The way that you relate to those around you and the energy that you reproduce will dictate the way that those around you relate to you and the energy that is circulated back to you.

LOVE AND LET GO

Society taught us that love is possessive. Your goal must be to love a person until they become free.

GIVE AND YOU SHALL RECEIVE

Be so concerned with giving back to the universe that it willfully gives back to you.

A WEALTHY MINDSET

If you don't come from a wealthy family, allow a wealthy family to come from you.

LAW AND ORDER

Respect the laws of the land and keep watch of the laws of man.

GUN

G: GOD
U: Universe
N: Nature

24 HOUR BALANCE

8 hours are for rest.
8 hours are for work.
8 hours are for everything else.

Society tells us to sleep when you are dead. If you lack rest, then you never rejuvenate, which also means that your mind, and body is always in motion. Before his untimely demise, Steve Jobs noted that we must consider what we demand of ourselves. Our time must be divided strategically to replenish and add value to the hours gifted to us each day. If your work takes precedence and your family takes precedence, then when will your time alotted for rest receive your attention? It is possible that an attempt to make everything of equal importance at the same time is a disservice to the hours in your day. Designating specific hours for specific activities and utilizing them in accordance with their designations can empower you to thrive and not just survive.

THE REAL BAG

Would you chase money if you knew that inner peace was the real bag?

LET YOUR SOUL GLOW

Toxic thought creates toxic healing and toxic manifestations.

CHARITIST

The words *Philanthropy* and *Charity* combined led me to create the term Charitist. The fusion of these two words combined highlight the importance of both. A philanthropist often contributes from a fiscal position and a person who works with or for a charity is often in the trenches performing the daily tasks of an organization's mission. When you do both of these acts, you can now be deemed a *Charitist* which consists of both principles.

RUN AND TELL THAT

Black lives, white lives, and blue lives aren't what matters. Spiritual and celestial lives matter.

WITTY ARE WE?

If you try to out wit yourself, you will most often end up without.

PERSONAL BUSINESS

Some say that business shouldn't be taken personally. The real truth is that business is always personal when it is handled by persons.

REIGN

Your opinion has no dominion. Facts are the solid foundation which structures are built upon.

THE SUN WILL COME OUT

You will never experience your tomorrows if you keep killing your todays.

A BIRD'S EYE VIEW

If you close your eyes, you can open your heart to see God with your 3rd eye.

THE PLEASURE PRINCIPLE

Why does purpose lead to pleasure, but pleasure does not lead to purpose?

IMAGINE THAT

Have you convinced yourself that your image is based on who others believe that you are?

REAL RECOGNIZES REAL

Is there a difference between your reality and the reality?

THE SHAPE

How is it that your hair is perpendicular, but your spirit is flat?

A QUEEN INDEED

Can you be a queen from the Motherland, but wear hair from another land?

STAND CORRECTED

Don't always assume that correction is equivalent to rejection.

PROGRAMMING & BELIEFS

All of our beliefs are as a result of the entities in which we are exposed. These entities can include but are not limited to:

- Television
- Radio
- Social Media
- Print Media
- Pop Culture
- Hip Hop Culture
- Religion
- Music

All of these entities are consumed through specific vehicles, those often being Religion and Television. The consumption of religion and television form our sets of beliefs. In the middle of all three of these words (Be{LIE}f, Re{LI}gion, and Te{LIE}vision) the word LIE is present. We should seek the truth and the truth should set us free. If we aren't free in our thinking it's often because we have been LIED to.

HOLIDAYS

Holiday should really be holy days, but because most pagan holidays are based off of fiction not fact they in turn aren't holy. This train is prevalent in examples such as the Easter Bunny. We are all aware of the fact that rabbits don't lay eggs, chickens do.

Also consider that if you scrambled the letters in the word Santa it could also create SATAN.

Consider the entity in which you worship and the information that compells you do adopt this information as your universal truth.

WORSHIP THE SOURCE NOT THE RESOURCE

Remember to worship the source not the resource. The source is the creator of all things. This also means that our greatest resources are derivatives of the source. Instead of opting to worship the sun, moon, or the stars, consider worshiping the creator of all.

To worship THE CREATOR is to worship all things verses worshiping THE CREATIVE, which only encompasses a few.

SWEAT

Sweat from our eyes is the soul/spirit crying. Sweat from the body is fat crying. When your body is purging, sweat and tears become the by product.

When you cry, your soul is purging. Consider tears as power. Your body is releasing spiritual toxins.

MISUNDERSTANDING

The term *misunderstanding* is not a word, it's an event. Understanding came looking for you but you missed it. The reason you missed it is because you were *under* the influence of alternative programming. The only way for understanding to find you is for you to recondition your mind to be awakened and alert to discovering truth.

Epilogue: Empty Minds Must Be Filled

> Whoever controls the ideas that are adopted as universal truths, controls the thinking; and whoever controls the thinking, controls the actions that result from those thoughts.
>
> — Stevie Briggs, Jr.

HAVE YOU EVER considered why people are relentless when killing animals, but question themselves when attempting to kill insects? It is often said that people die from a lack of knowledge. I would argue that people die from a lack of the exercise of acquired knowledge which in turn is wisdom. There are many concepts and ideas that you know but fail to exercise in your best interest. You must ask yourself…What, then, will you do with the knowledge that you have acquired? How will you use it to elevate your life and illuminate your path? My experience has taught me that not everyone will make the decision to be wise, but there are a select few who desire to live life amidst an awakening that validates the information extended in this book as truth. Will you empty your mind to refill it with your truths according to your experiences and the wisdom that you have acquired?

Your life and your journey are yours for the taking. Your habits, the information that you receive into your cache, your experiences and your will determine what will manifest in your life. The most critical action that you can take is to free your mind and make room for deprogramming and reprogramming. Take the necessary measures to unlearn information that you no longer wish to adopt as your universal truth and replenish it with powerful tools that filter and fulfill your higher calling. Fill your mind, body and spirit with truths that edify and empowr you. Your universal truth is that you hold the key to unlock the information that leads to your destiny. Will you use it?

If there were a reward for speaking *truth* more people would. Those who do so recognize that to be *awakened* is the reward.

— Stevie Briggs, Jr.

Afterword: Opened Minds Open Doors

HE OR SHE who is raised in an indigenous environment or on a farm, will have a different perspective than one who grew up in the city. Exposure and experiences shape perspective and truth. You have been exposed when you've experienced something—that's your truth, but that doesn't mean it's a UNIVERSAL TRUTH. Consider the concept of gravity, it is a universal truth. The way that it works and how it is defined is true for all. No matter the perspective, the concept of gravity will be consistent. This is an example of a UNIVERAL TRUTH.

We must not only recognize and adopt the UNIVERSAL TRUTH as our own but also acknowledge the moments of our lives when we may be asleep and unaware of the universal truths around us. It is not possible for us to keep doing the same things and expecting different results. One might say that they no longer wish to be overweight, but if they continue to consume the same foods that led to the weight gain, the problem will persist. Assuming new levels of consciousness denotes that you are able to unlearn and relearn your truths, the truths of others and more importantly, the UNIVERSAL TRUTHS.

I used to own a restaurant and on certain days I hosted a social meeting called "Conscious Conversation". During these meetings we discussed the following five power structures: political, economical, social, educational, and spiritual. The conversations compelled us to dig deeper into what these five power structures affected the execution of our daily lives and journey towards consciousness. We ventured to turn the term politics into *Poli-*

tricks. We considered that there was a right wing and a left wing but each wing was still attached to one bird. We also discussed the realization that economics was a tool to make society spend money on frivolous things instead of functional needs alone. These conversations empowered us to recognize that we were fighting a war on economics and ideas rather than a war on race. However, the social structure has placed clubs, associations, religions, fraternities and sororities into the rotations of our lives to seperate us. Consider the fact that the only way that one can steal, kill and destroy you is if you are seperated. Where there is unity there is strength and peace.

We also discussed the concept of education. Education is not meant to educate you, it was created to assess and separate you. If you are an AP or an honors student, you have one designation. If you are a student at a magnet school, then you could have another designation. If you are classified as having SLD or ADHD or you have been diagnosed as Autistic, then there is a different placement assigned.

We don't often speak about the credit cycle as students matriculate through elementary school, high school, and college. I find it ironic we don't talk about this system in traditional school systems, yet it is everything that we need to know to acquire home ownership in this country. This concept should be something that we teach our children to ensure their success. FICO scores were created in 1956 by William R. Fair and Earl Judson Issac. Lenders at banks could use the scores to determine if a potential buyer was worthy of having credit extended from the bank. These individuals recognized that banks would not be able to discriminate against a person solely from their social security number. After asking for a home address, it was easier to incite discrimanatory practices based on zip codes. If a zip code's median income was $60,580, but the income is $50,580, that gives a tremendous amount of insight as to how much liquid cash might be available to a potential borrower. Additionally, each zip code denoted a certain type of residency that was also taken into consideration. These practices are still intact today and prevent many people from realizing the goal of home ownership. A lack of knowledge of this system is one measure taken to ensure that people are docile and unable to get financial liberty and freedom. We are not fighting a war on race, we are fighting a war on economics and classism.

All of these structures are put in place to keep you separated. This is why I always tell people that we don't live in a community, we live in a neighborhood. In a community, there is the presence of unity. When you examine a community, people control their food, their education, economics, and their policing. We don't live in communities anymore, we live in neighborhoods. Consider the person wearing a hood. Their vision is not as clear as it could be becuase the periphial is obstructed. You don't have full access to the surrounding areas. This same concept is likened to the truth about communities versus neighborhoods. It is not until you put down the hood that you unveil the truth.

The problem with this is, most people feel we are fighting a war on race when we are fighting a war on economics. When you know the power of it, you're able to maneuver so that you always win. To sleep is detrimental because you don't notice the origin of it.

Racism is one of the biggest distractions created to prohibit us from discovering truth. One of my mentors taught me that the war is not against your *color*, it is against your *kind*. That is the destruction piece that we must be awakened to recognize and defeat and all costs.

Postscript: Unwrapping the Gift of Curiosity

IN THE COMPOSITION of this book, I have arrived at a place of unprecedented peace. This level of existing would not be possible if I were concerned with the notion that not everyone will endeavour to wake up. In this space, I must be in silent agreement with the fact that not every person has reached a stage in their journey that they desire to unwrap the gift of curiosity. What I can ascertain is that those who do will know that I carry this torch, unapologetically that we might never be asleep on the people, places, and information that stretches our parameters and forces us to journey towards the unchartered territory of our minds, hearts and existence. We have all been called to infinite greatness that bears no limits but simply existing and serving as a retainer of the same messaging that was created to oppress will not miraculously result in ascension. I want to see you soar and to give up every piece of information and practice that has been established to weigh you down. The world has not given you your spirit, don't let the world take it away. Ask questions about everything and use the power of your thoughts to transform the way that you show up and engage in the world. You were called for a time such as this. You were called to be WOKE!

Consciousness is the real revolution.

— Stevie Briggs, Jr.

Woke 360

WE MUST REMAIN in constant pursuit of empowerment, abundance and elevation to vibrate at the highest levels possible while evolving. The Woke 360 Community serve as the incubator that breeds prosperity in all facets of life. Our approach to this end denotes a consistent flow of education and enlightenment in the following areas:

- Political
- Social
- Economic
- Education
- Spirit

This program has been established to ensure that the people never perish from a lack of knowledge.

For more information about how you can join the *Woke 360 Community* visit

WWW.STEVIEBAGGSJR.COM

Woke 360

Although society has given us a variety of tools that serve to program our minds, bodies and spirits, we must recognize and apply essential acts that counter those messages with the spirit and consciousness such that we vibrate on higher levels. The evolution of elevation will always be the goal. This 21 Day Challenge, focuses on applying the art of manifestation to specific areas of your life. We will begin this process by leveraging the power of affirmations and intention. Always remember that you rightfullly have access to all the power that you will ever need.

Days 1-7

Intention

MENTAL & EMOTIONAL FREEDOM

DAY 1: I CELEBRATE MYSELF IN THIS DAY BY
_____
_____
_____
_____
_____
_____
_____

DAY 2: I WILL RAISE MY VIBRATION BY

_____

_____

_____

_____

_____

DAY 3: I WILL ELIMINATE NEGATIVE PATTERNS OF THINKING BY

_____

_____

_____

_____

_____

DAY 4: I WILL ENVISION MY PROSPERITY BY

_____

_____

_____

_____

_____

DAY 5: I WILL ELEVATE MY LEVELS OF THINKING BY

_____

_____

_____

_____

_____

DAY 6: I WILL TEACH SOMEONE A NEW CONCEPT TO FREE THEIR MINDS

_____

_____

_____

_____

_____

DAY 7: I WILL MANIFEST MY BIRTHRIGHT OF EXCELLENCE BY

_____

_____

_____

_____

_____

To be physically strong is to be mentally and spiritually *strengthened*.

Days 8-14

Intention

PHYSICAL FREEDOM

DAY 8: I WILL HONOR MY TEMPLE BY

_____

_____

_____

_____

_____

_____

_____

DAY 9: I WILL ELIMINATE THE USE OF TOXINS IN MY BODY BY

_____
_____
_____
_____
_____

DAY 10: I WILL EXERT EVIDENCE OF MY PHYSICAL STRENGTH BY

_____
_____
_____
_____
_____

DAY 11: I WILL EMPOWER SOMEONE AROUND ME TO RECOGNIZE THEIR PHYSICAL STRENGTH BY

_____

_____

_____

_____

DAY 12: I WILL CONQUER A NEW PHYSICAL CHALLENGE ACTIVITY BY

_____

_____

_____

_____

DAY 13: I WILL REPROGRAM MY MIND TO ACHIEVE NEW PHYSICAL RESULTS BY

_____

_____

_____

_____

_____

DAY 14: I WILL STRENGTHEN MY BODY BY

_____

_____

_____

_____

The *wealth* of the universe hastens *towards* me.

Days 15-21

Intention

FINANCIAL FREEDOM

DAY 15: I WILL MAKE ROOM FOR WEALTH IN MY LIFE BY

_____
_____
_____
_____
_____
_____
_____

DAY 16: I WILL ELIMINATE MY FEARS ABOUT FINANCES BY

_____

_____

_____

_____

_____

DAY 17: I WILL EMPOWER MYSELF THROUGH MY FINANCES BY

_____

_____

_____

_____

_____

DAY 18: I WILL EMPOWER THOSE AROUND ME THROUGH MY FINANCES BY

_____

_____

_____

_____

DAY 19: I WILL SOW A FINANCIAL SEED IN MY COMMUNITY BY

_____

_____

_____

_____

DAY 20: I WILL PURSUE NEW FINANCIAL OPPORTUNITIES BY

_____
_____
_____
_____
_____

DAY 21: I WILL CHANGE THE WAY I THINK ABOUT WEALTH BY

_____
_____
_____
_____
_____

About the Author

The Athlete. Many know Stevie Baggs, Jr. for his athletic career as a three-time All-American linebacker, playing in both the NFL and CFL, for teams including the Baltimore Ravens, Arizona Cardinals, Saskatchewan Roughriders, and Hamilton Tiger-Cats. During his college football career, Stevie Baggs Jr. earned his nickname, "Shakespeare", by making plays on and off the field. He graduated in 2005 with a degree in International Business from Bethune Cookman University.

The Inspirational Speaker. Drawing from his experience in professional sports, Stevie Baggs Jr. has dedicated time in his career to empowering youth and adults as an international inspirational speaker. His driven attitude and gracious service to the community has gained him the support and partnership of many renowned charitable, educational, health and sports organizations. Named Health and Wellness Ambassador for the City of Atlanta by Mayor Kasim Reed, Stevie continues to be a strong voice for the promotion of a healthy lifestyle.

The Actor /Entrepreneur. Stevie can be spotted on the big screen, having worked alongside Will Smith in the movie, "Focus." You may have seen him on the hit TV show, "STAR" on FOX, and on his own show, "A Match Made in Heaven" on WEtv. In addition to his acting endeavors, Stevie Baggs, Jr. has made TV appearances on The Steve Harvey Show, The Wendy Williams Show, and The View. He is also an Ambassador for Young Living Essential Oils.

The Philanthropist. As an advocate for change, Stevie Baggs, Jr. works in communities to enhance the minds of youth to fuel the future through his CETA (Creating Empowerment Through Autonomy) foundation. The CETA Foundation, currently celebrating 17 years of service, envisions a world where all individuals have the health and wellness tools, resources, and support to maximize their quality of life.

The Author. Recognized as the only athlete to play for eleven professional teams in ten years, "Shakespeare" continues to inspire and make plays off the field. In his bestselling book, "Greater than the Game," Baggs shares how his experiences on the field prepared him for purpose beyond the stadium and guides readers to self-discovery by challenging them to examine how they can elevate their personal "game." As a man of many hats, Stevie continues to execute his destiny with an unwavering heart of leadership and service. With all that he does, he often says, "I'm not flawless, but I am faithful."

I believe that we have an *obligation* to teach the masses what we learn throughout our lives. We must also *endeavor* to teach what we have learned to further perpetuate the continuous elevation of the *world* around us.

— Stevie Briggs, Jr.

Connect with Stevie Baggs, Jr. on Social Media

FACEBOOK www.facebook.com/steviebaggs

TWITTER @steviebaggsjr

INSTAGRAM @steviebaggsjr

PRESS, MEDIA AND SPEAKING BOOKINGS:
bookings@steviebaggsjr.com